The Dolphin Family

 CHELSEA CLUBHOUSE

An Imprint of Chelsea House Publishers
A Haights Cross Communications Company
Philadelphia

Bev Harvey

This edition first published in 2004 in the United States of America by Chelsea Clubhouse, a division of Chelsea House Publishers and a subsidiary of Haights Cross Communications.

Chelsea Clubhouse
1974 Sproul Road, Suite 400
Broomall, PA 19008-0914

The Chelsea House world wide web address is www.chelseahouse.com

Library of Congress Cataloging-in-Publication Data

Harvey, Bev.
   The dolphin family / Bev Harvey.
   p. cm. — (Animal families)
   Summary: Simple text compares and contrasts members of the dolphin family in terms of
   where they live, body features, eating habits, and size.
   ISBN 0-7910-7543-5
   1. Delphinidae—Juvenile literature. [1. Dolphin family (Mammals) 2. Dolphins.] I. Title. II. Series.
   QL737.C432H37 2004
   599.53—dc21

                                                              2002155659

First published in 2003 by
MACMILLAN EDUCATION AUSTRALIA PTY LTD
627 Chapel Street, South Yarra, Australia, 3141

Associated companies and representatives throughout the world.

Copyright © Bev Harvey 2003
Copyright in photographs © individual photographers as credited

Edited by Angelique Campbell-Muir
Page layout by Domenic Lauricella
Photo research by Sarah Saunders

Printed in China

Acknowledgements

The author and the publisher are grateful to the following for permission to reproduce copyright material:

Cover photograph: spotted dolphin, courtesy of ANT Photo Library.

ANT Photo Library, pp. 1, 11, 15, 16; Andrea Florence/Ardea, pp. 7 (top), 22, 23; Mark Carwardine—Still Pictures/Auscape, pp. 8–9; Jean-Paul Ferrero/Auscape, p. 21; François Gohier/Auscape, pp. 6 (top), 14; D. Parer & E. Parer-Cook/Auscape, p. 26; Doug Perrine/Auscape, pp. 10, 17; Tui De Roy/Auscape, p. 5; Robin W. Baird, p. 25; Graeme Cresswell/Bio-Images, pp. 7 (center), 24; Eva Boogaard/Lochman Transparencies, p. 18; Jiri Lochman/Lochman Transparencies, pp. 4 (top), 6 (center), 19; Kelvin Aitken/Marine Themes, pp. 4 (bottom), 28, 29; Photolibrary.com, pp. 7 (bottom), 27; Jean Pierre Sylvestre, pp. 6 (bottom), 20.

While every care has been taken to trace and acknowledge copyright, the publisher tenders their apologies for any accidental infringement where copyright has proved untraceable. Where the attempt has been unsuccessful, the publisher welcomes information that would redress the situation.

Contents

Animal Families

Scientists group similar kinds of animals together. They call these groups families. The animals that belong to each family share similar features.

smooth waterproof skin

blowhole

small eyes

flippers

blowhole

smooth waterproof skin

flippers

The dolphin family

All kinds of dolphins belong to the dolphin family. **Marine** dolphins live all over the world in oceans and seas. A few can also live in rivers. Dolphins are not fish. They are **mammals**. They come to the water's surface to breathe air.

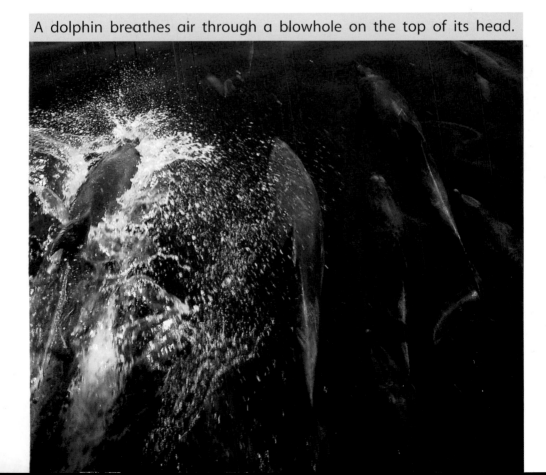
A dolphin breathes air through a blowhole on the top of its head.

Where Dolphins Live

Common dolphins are found in warm and tropical waters in the Atlantic and Pacific Oceans.

Bottlenose dolphins are common in cool, warm, and tropical waters in the Atlantic, Indian, and Pacific Oceans.

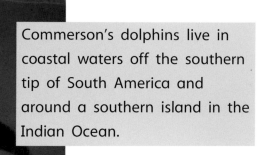

Commerson's dolphins live in coastal waters off the southern tip of South America and around a southern island in the Indian Ocean.

Tucuxi river dolphins live in coastal waters and deep river areas of eastern Central America and northeastern South America.

Northern right whale dolphins swim in the deep, cool waters of the northern Pacific Ocean.

Killer whales roam all oceans and seas. They are found both in deep waters and near coasts.

Dolphin Features

Members of the dolphin family have many of these features in common.

flippers for swimming, leaping, and diving

a blowhole for breathing

a large brain

a beak with many teeth for eating fish

small ears behind its eyes

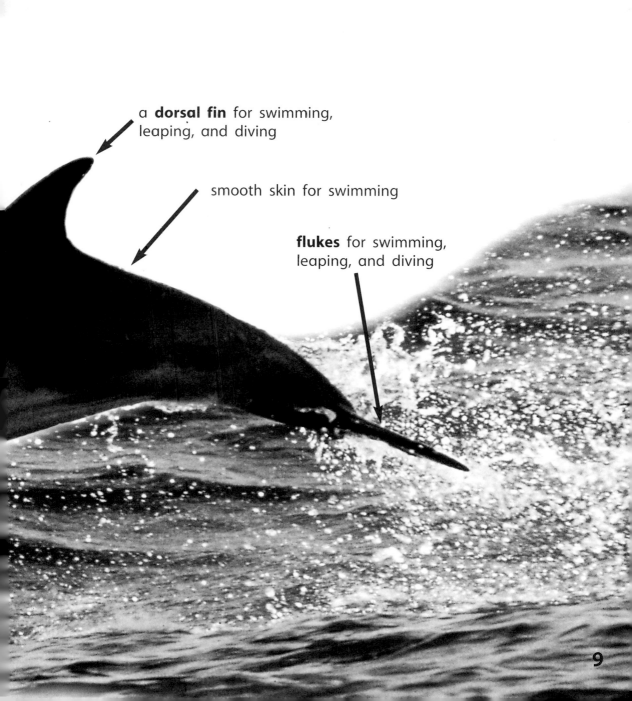

a **dorsal fin** for swimming, leaping, and diving

smooth skin for swimming

flukes for swimming, leaping, and diving

9

Dolphins as Hunters

Dolphins are fast swimmers. They often travel by diving in and out of the water.

A dolphin uses its tail to push it forward and to jump out of the water.

Most dolphins hunt and eat fish.

Dolphins are **carnivores**, which means they eat meat. Most dolphins catch fish and squid to eat. They make a clicking sound that **echoes** off objects in the sea. Dolphins listen for the echoes to find **schools** of fish to hunt.

The Size of Dolphins

Some dolphins are big. Some dolphins are small. The killer whale is the biggest member of the dolphin family.

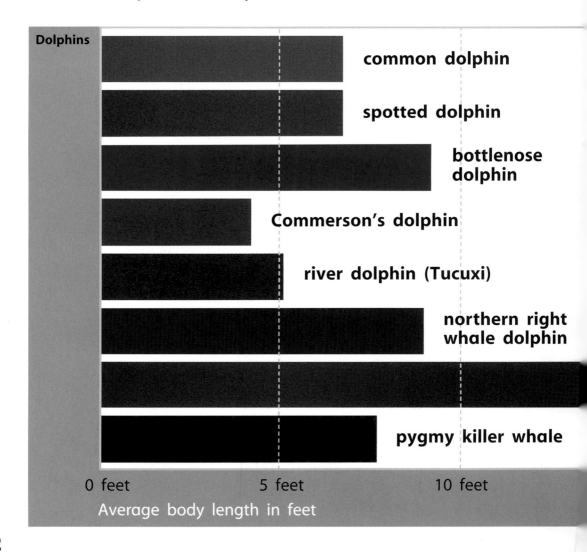

Dolphins

common dolphin

spotted dolphin

bottlenose dolphin

Commerson's dolphin

river dolphin (Tucuxi)

northern right whale dolphin

pygmy killer whale

0 feet   5 feet   10 feet

Average body length in feet

Dolphins are measured from the tip of the beak to the end of the tail.

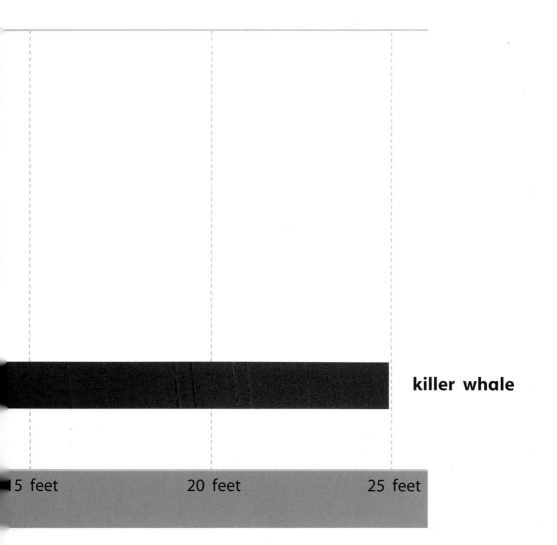

killer whale

5 feet   20 feet   25 feet

Common Dolphins

The common dolphin lives in a large school. It swims, eats, and breathes with the other dolphins in its school.

At times, whole schools of common dolphins will come to the surface together to breathe.

Dolphins make noises to communicate with each other.

Common dolphins are dark on top and light underneath. Their sides have light patches. Like other dolphins, they communicate with whistles and clicks.

Spotted Dolphins

The young spotted dolphin does not have spots. The spots appear as it grows older.

This young dolphin will get spots as it grows older.

A spotted dolphin has dark spots on its underside and light spots on its back.

The spotted dolphin is a fast swimmer. It can swim at more than 15 miles (25 kilometers) an hour. It can leap high out of the water.

Bottlenose Dolphins

The bottlenose dolphin has a large brain. Some scientists work with these dolphins to measure their intelligence.

Bottlenose dolphins are large dolphins with a shorter beak.

Some bottlenose dolphins are friendly toward humans.

Sailors often see bottlenose dolphins swimming beside their ships. In some places bottlenose dolphins come close to shore to be with humans.

Commerson's Dolphins

Commerson's dolphin is small and **stocky**. It has a rounded dorsal fin and no beak.

Commerson's dolphins are black and white.

One nickname for this type of dolphin is skunk dolphin.

The Commerson's dolphin looks for waves to play on. It rides as the waves break on the shore or in the wind. It sometimes rides on the waves made by ships.

River Dolphins (Tucuxi)

The Tucuxi (say too-koo-shee) is a dolphin that lives along the coast in the bays and mouths of large rivers. It can live in fresh or salt water.

The Tucuxi is one of the smallest marine dolphins.

Many Tucuxi dolphins live near the mouth of the Amazon river in South America.

The Tucuxi usually glides smoothly to the surface of the water. It often breathes through its blowhole without leaping out of the water.

Northern Right Whale Dolphins

The northern right whale dolphin is black with a white belly. It does not have a dorsal fin.

The northern right whale dolphin does not have a fin on its back.

Northern right whale dolphins have small flippers and small flukes.

It lives in cool, deep waters away from the coast. Up to 3,000 northern right whale dolphins have been seen swimming together.

Killer Whales

The killer whale lives in a **pod** of up to 40 whales. A pod is usually led by a large female. Most members of a pod are related to each other.

The dorsal fin of a male killer whale can be 6 feet (1.8 meters) tall.

Killer whales sometimes hunt seals near shore.

The killer whale eats mainly fish. Killer whales
will sometimes hunt together in a pod to
catch much bigger **prey** like seals and whales.

27

Pygmy Killer Whales

The pygmy killer whale is much smaller than the killer whale. The pygmy killer whale is a powerful hunter. It catches large fish, squid, and octopus to eat.

A pygmy killer whale has a rounded head.

Pygmy killer whales usually live in deep waters away from the coast.

The pygmy killer whale charges at its prey, biting and snapping at it. The growl of the pygmy killer whale is so loud it can be heard out of the water.

Common and Scientific Names

The scientific name for the marine dolphin family is Delphinidae. There are 32 types of dolphins in this family. These are the common and scientific names of the ones in this book:

Delphinidae family		
Common name	**Scientific names:**	
	Genus	**Species**
common dolphin	*Delphinus*	*delphis*
spotted dolphin	*Stenella*	*attenuata*
bottlenose dolphin	*Tursiops*	*truncatus*
Commerson's dolphin	*Cephalorhynchus*	*commersonii*
river dolphin (Tucuxi)	*Sotalia*	*fluviatilis*
northern right whale dolphin	*Lissodelphis*	*borealis*
killer whale	*Orcinus*	*orca*
pygmy killer whale	*Feresa*	*attenuata*

The Delphinidae family members described in this book all live in oceans or seas. Most river dolphins are members of other scientific families.

Glossary

carnivores	animals that eat meat
dorsal fin	the fin on a dolphin's back
echoes	sounds that bounce back after hitting an object
flukes	the two halves of a dolphin's tail
genus	the name for a large group of similar animals within an animal family; the genus is the first part of the scientific name of an animal
mammals	animals that breathe air and feed milk to their young
marine	having to do with the ocean
pod	a group of marine animals; pods usually refer to smaller groups than schools.
prey	an animal that is hunted for food
schools	large groups of marine animals; there can be thousands of fish or dolphins in a school.
species	a group of animals that are closely related and can produce young; the species is the second part of the scientific name of an animal
stocky	short and thick looking

Index